SHAMANIC CRYSTALS ORACLE

A GUIDE TO SUPPORT YOUR PERSONAL WORK
AND SOUL AWAKENING

BARBARA MARCHI

Artwork by Cristina Fontana

Copyright © 2024 Barbara Marchi
Artwork Copyright © 2024 Cristina Fontana

All rights reserved. Other than for personal use, no part of these cards or this book may be reproduced in any way, in whole or part, without the written consent of the copyright holder or publisher. This publication is intended for spiritual and emotional guidance only. The content is not intended to replace medical assistance or treatment. The views and opinions expressed by the author, both within and outside of this publication, do not necessarily reflect the views of the publisher.

Published by Blue Angel Publishing®
10 Trafford Court, Wheelers Hill,
Victoria, Australia 3150
E-mail: info@blueangelonline.com
Website: www.blueangelonline.com

Translated by Cristina Oliva

Edited by Peter Loupelis & Jules Sutherland

Blue Angel is a registered trademark of Blue Angel Gallery Pty Ltd.

ISBN: 978-1-922574-21-3

ACKNOWLEDGMENT

A deep sense of gratitude rises from my heart, and for that, I dedicate this oracle to the deep feeling of my soul, to the sky, the earth, and the universe for sending these messages of light.

I extend my dedication to the soul of Cristina Fontana, the artist, who created these wonderful drawings with an open heart, to the soul of Cristina Oliva, my publisher and translator, for believing in this project. I also offer my thanks to my friends and family for their continued help and support.

Finally, this oracle is for all of you, souls on your journey, that it may become a guide for your lives.

TABLE OF CONTENTS

INTRODUCTION 7
Working with the Shamanic Crystals Oracle 10
Purifying the Oracle 12
Card Spreads 12

CRYSTAL SPIRIT CARD MESSAGES 21
AMAZONITE 22
AMETHYST 25
ANGELITE 28
APOPHYLLITE 31
AVENTURINE 34
BLACK TOURMALINE 36
BLUE CHALCEDONY 39
BLUE–GREEN LABRADORITE 42
BOTSWANA AGATE 45
CARNELIAN 47
CELESTINE 50
CHRYSOCOLLA 53
CITRINE QUARTZ 56
GARNET 59
HEMATITE 61
HERKIMER 64
HYALINE QUARTZ 67
KYANITE 70
LAPIS LAZULI 73
MALACHITE 76
MOONSTONE 79

MOSS AGATE **82**
OCEAN JASPER **85**
PETRIFIED WOOD **88**
RAINBOW FLUORITE **91**
RED JASPER **94**
RHODONITE **97**
ROSE QUARTZ **100**
RUTILATED QUARTZ **103**
SAPPHIRE **106**
SELENITE **109**
SMOKY QUARTZ **111**
SNOWFLAKE OBSIDIAN **114**
SODALITE **117**
SUNSTONE **119**
TIGER'S EYE **122**
TOURMALINATED QUARTZ **125**
TURQUOISE **128**
WATERMELON TOURMALINE **131**
WHITE LABRADORITE **134**

THE DIRECTIONS CARD MESSAGES 137
EASTERN DIRECTION **138**
NORTHERN DIRECTION **140**
SOUTHERN DIRECTION **142**
WESTERN DIRECTION **144**
WHITE FEATHER **146**

About the Author **149**
About the Artist **151**

INTRODUCTION

WELCOME TO ALL THE DEAR SOULS WHO, WITH GREAT curiosity, have heard the call of this oracle.

The crystal guides conveyed messages to me that were immediate and clear, an immense gift that inspired me, from the very beginning, to share them with other radiant souls.

The first time I held a drum, I touched its skin with my fingers and could feel the ancestral power of this sacred and ancient instrument on me. My very first shamanic journey was unexpectedly clear, along with the message that my guides brought me that day — creating the *Shamanic Crystals Oracle*.

Seven years passed since that time, but the oracle had been waiting an even longer time to manifest into reality. Although the crystal guides flooded my heart with joy, I was by no means ready then. The years flew by quickly as I justified not coming to terms with this work. My insecurities, not feeling up to it, fear of judgment, and the shadows of my personality (you know what I'm talking about, right?) left the precious dream and bright intent of bringing this project to life in a corner of my heart. In spite of everything, I am grateful for what time taught me, giving me the opportunity to break down those limitations that held back my soul, so that it was free to express itself and speak peacefully. It was not always easy and automatic to strip back the many layers that covered it. There were moments of momentum followed by more intense moments of total blockage in which I was really good at playing the role of the monkeys who don't speak, see, or hear.

One day, a friend I had not seen in a long time, a precious soul with many gifts, arrived. She said, "I am here because I have a message from Heaven to give you. Take back who you are and put it to service. Heaven loves you, take care of your heart and trust what you feel." At that moment, besides being speechless, my heart vibrated stronger and exploded with joy.

From an early age I felt and cultivated a hunger for knowledge. Not canonical, academic knowledge, but knowledge of the soul. I attended classes and met therapists. I was thrilled, and at the same time, very fragile and manipulable. I was slowly opening doors of old wounds, which I was not always enthusiastic and willing to observe. I was accompanied by good teachers, met fantastic and inspiring people — but I also met teachers who made me hate the holistic world at times because of how they used their charisma and knowledge in an unbecoming way.

After so many lived experiences, however, I realized that I really had to figure who I wanted to be without stubbornly focusing on one particular practice or current of thought. That is when something authentic in me clicked. With this awareness I felt a deep need to follow the way of my heart and my memories. I now walk the path—which is definitely long—with more lightness, curiosity, and without fear.

I am excited to continue my work of growth and evolution, and to discover and remove some more heavy, crystallized layers, because it allows me to explore the infinite zones of being. And often, it is fun to do so!

I thought telling a part of my experience might be helpful to you, especially if you have gone or are going through similar situations. Always put your trust in yourself and your heart without falling into temptation. Don't put someone else on a pedestal simply because you feel unsure of yourself — listen to what is authentically moving within you. There is immense beauty waiting for you. When facing personal challenges, trust that you are capable of overcoming them by taking the right steps. They will lead you to your growth and evolution, making your soul lighter and free to fly high.

Thank you, dear soul, for reading my words.
Barbara

WORKING WITH THE *SHAMANIC CRYSTALS ORACLE*

The crystal animal worlds, along with the celestial and earth guides, are great allies and messengers that help you on your journey and awaken important memories. They embody and represent, dear soul, the countless facets that are part of you, your qualities, your resources, and also your limitations. Remember that crystals work within you because they are part of you — minerals are present and essential in human physiology. The animal spirit, on the other hand, is intrinsically linked to your primordial and ancient essence. Heavenly and earthly spirits live in a dimension unseen by human eyes, touching your heart and its divine memory.

These cards serve as a means for self-reflection, delving into your profound inner layers, and are sure to resonate with significant inner aspects, inspiring your personal development and advancement. The deck consists of 45 cards, comprising 40 spirits of crystals and animals, four spirits of the directions, and a card represented by the spirit of the white feather. Please use them respectfully and responsibly, taking the proper time to listen to what they want to communicate to you.

What I have always liked about the study of crystals and shamanism is that they do not respond to any human laws, but only to the natural and universal ones present on Heaven and Earth. Since the beginning of time, everything has taken shape according to a harmonious and balanced rhythm. Every movement is guided by an intelligent flow of higher energy. Everything possesses equal value, and no one is excluded, regardless of their form. Everything is connected in constant communication at a deep level. The animal, plant, and crystalline worlds move through time by following the weather, temperatures, and the water cycle. The orbit around the sun and our moon's orbit of the planet create a natural, biological clock.

We have lost this natural rhythm. Modern society has come to impose an order that is not balanced with the natural rhythms, causing countless problems and disconnecting our spirits from Mother Earth and Father Sky.

Through using this oracle, you will experience how much energy you have at your disposal, and how all the natural elements of this world are great allies at your service, to help you discover who you really are. And all this with immense, unconditional love. The whole universe wants only the best for you.

PURIFYING THE ORACLE

Before using these cards, cleanse the deck of any residual energy it may have accumulated during production, with incense (any incense you already have is fine) or even simply with an intention. You can repeat this process periodically as you see fit, following your intuition.

At this point, bless the cards by thanking them, asking for their alliance, and that they may be an instrument of truth for your highest good.

CARD SPREADS

Four-Directions Spread
This spread can be a good way to know what kind of energy you are embodying in the present, regardless of whatever you are going through. It can be helpful to do this kind of reading during the passage of a solstice or equinox, as these are special days charged with energy and natural magic.

The four directions correspond to the four seasons, representing the stages of life we go through, as we develop in years and personal awareness.

EAST — SPRING
SOUTH — SUMMER
WEST — AUTUMN
NORTH — WINTER

Time flows perpetually, regardless of our will and control. It becomes precious only when we are conscious of it. This spread is useful when you wish to ask a question along the lines of, "What phase of life am I going through right now?"

At this point, take the four Directions cards from the deck, shuffle them while you breathe calmly, and lay them side by side, turned face down. Choose the one that resonates most and turn it over. Read the directions for awareness and ritualizing this moment.

If you wish to have an additional tool, ask, "Which crystal will support and guide me in this phase?"

Take the rest of the cards, shuffle them well, and breathe. Lay them all out horizontally, one next to the other face down. Pass your hand or gaze softly at the cards. When you feel ready, pick up a card and read the message.

The Daily Spread

The sun corresponds with the present, masculine energy, the fire element, 'doing', and the energy that flows through us. Whenever we ask the oracles for daily advice, we are tapping into this energy. You can use this spread to ask for a message for the day or for anything else you need direction on.

I recommend that you always ask clear, open-ended questions, ones that you can't answer with a 'yes' or 'no'. For example, instead of asking, "Will I get the job I am interviewing for?" ask instead, "How is this job going to be good for me?" This allows a conversation to happen between yourself and your guides, via the cards.

Consider your question. Shuffle all 45 cards, and take a deep breath, bringing your awareness to your heart. If you wish, you can light a candle or incense to help you get in deeper, intimate contact with your divine essence.

When you feel you have shuffled enough, fan the cards out, face down. Now, instinctively draw a card, which represents the answer to your question. I recommend you take a minute to look at it closely. Tune in to what it says to you directly. Then read the entry for it in this guidebook.

The Sun's Illumination Spread

If, on the other hand, you want a broader, more detailed reading about what your soul is going through, and how best to deal with the challenges, let the sun shine its light to illuminate what you need. For this spread, you only need the 40 Crystal Spirit cards.

Breathe deeply, shuffle the cards as you focus on your situation, and lay the cards face down. Intuitively choose three cards.

Card One: the situation you are coming from and your present moment

Card Two: the passage you are about to face

Card Three: the direction your soul wishes to take

After reading the meaning of the three cards, take another deep breath, close your eyes, and with intention and trust ask for the quality you can put into action to help you overcome the situation you are experiencing, and draw another card that calls you. **Card Four** will show you the crystal and animal guide that will accompany you. You can invoke them to help deal with this moment in your life.

Moon Spreads

The phases of the moon's cycle will be taken into consideration for the following spreads: the new (crescent) moon, waxing moon, full moon, and waning moon. Each of them embodies a different energy connected to feminine energy — introspective, enigmatic, magnetic, and somewhat veiled. The moon moves emotions, turns dreams into reality, and helps you improve who you are.

The New and Waxing Moon Spread

The new moon can be defined as a fresh start — the planting of a seed that becomes a new project or an updated approach to living your life. To ask the new moon for help is to tap into a deep energy, full of transformative magic. This movement will last throughout the crescent moon phase. Consulting the oracle on the day of the new moon is the perfect time for this spread.

Formulate your question or intention about what energy can help you develop something new. To celebrate this moment, you might like to light a red candle to symbolize abundance and focused planning. You can use incense to amplify your feeling, and to cleanse the sacred space where you live or work.

Take the 40 Crystal Spirit cards and shuffle them while repeating your question or intention in your mind three times. Arrange all the cards face down, breathe deeply, and let the card that strikes your eye guide you with an open heart. Alternatively, pass your hand over it until you feel the card calling you.

Draw four cards and arrange them in a half-moon shape with the tips facing east.

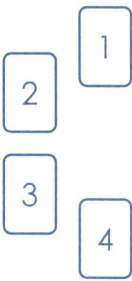

Choose one card from these four, always listening to the one that resonates most with you. This energy will be your ally and source of strength during the crescent moon phase, having your intention well in mind.

The Full Moon Spread

The full moon represents completeness, the magic of manifestation, and the confidence of fulfillment. On this magical night, celebrate with gratitude, faith, and listen to the profound messages that may come to you — let them be. Most importantly, bring your heart into a state of connection in which you feel you are part of the whole.

If you wish to use sacred objects to support this reading, incense will help purify your space and calm your mind, a white candle can enhance the power of light, and flowers or medicinal plants make beautiful offerings.

Remove the four Directions cards from the deck and shuffle the remaining 41 cards. Ask for a message that speaks of the present and presence.

Draw nine cards. Arrange eight of them in a circle face down. The ninth card will be in the center. Turn it over and be amazed at the message it has for you on this magical day.

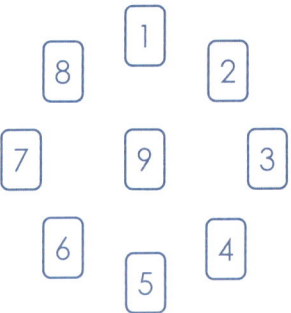

The Full and Waning Moon Spread

You have taken the time to plan and manifest, now it is time to clean up and let go of what no longer belongs to you. Honor this little death to be reborn lighter and more aware. Letting go is not easy, but this moon offers you a great opportunity.

Take advantage of the many nights of the waning moon, and when you feel ready, prepare a beautiful green candle representing lightness, burn some incense (such as ethically sourced palo santo or white sage) as a great ally of energetic cleansing, and consider your intention or something you would like to let go of.

Remove the four Directions cards as well as the White Feather card from the deck, leaving the 40 Crystal Spirit cards. Shuffle these and breathe deeply. As you exhale, let go of all physical and emotional tension.

Lay out all the cards in front of you by spreading them out face down while you focus on what you wish to leave behind. Observe with an open heart or run your hand over the cards until you draw out four that you will arrange in a semicircle, so that it depicts a half moon with the tips facing west.

Now, all you have to do is choose one of these four cards that will represent the energy of this moment. This is the crystal and animal spirit that will help you release all that no longer serves you.

CRYSTAL SPIRIT CARD MESSAGES

MAY THIS ORACLE PROVIDE YOU WITH DAILY opportunities to embrace the messages the guides intend for your highest good, allowing you to find joy in the gradual changes that will enhance your life.

Rest assured you are never alone. Cherish the beauty that shines within you. The energy released and transformed through the self-improvement work you choose to undertake will radiate outward, like the ripples in the water created by a stone cast into the sea of life — vast and everlasting waves that converge and unite until they form a single, powerful wave propelling change.

You are called to make your unmistakable and wonderful contribution to the world. You have a responsibility and a duty to yourself and others to make your gifts and talents available, for it would indeed be a shame not to show the light that shines from within you. Thank you, from heart to heart, to your soul simply for existing.

AMAZONITE

Follow with confidence the coincidences of life.

I AM THE SPIRIT OF THE AMAZONITE. WITH GREAT pride and gentleness, I am here to let you know you have a bold choice to make. You've misplaced your confidence and faith in life, as well as the divine design that Heaven—in collaboration with your soul—has scripted for your evolution.

Many good things happen in life, but so do bad things. We lose our way in the desire to survive because we find it difficult to understand certain events that occur. Disappointed, angry, and with low morale, we come to believe the idea that joy doesn't come easily, or that we should embrace it cautiously, fearing that something adverse might occur. Well, dear soul, I am here to strongly affirm that this is not the case. Nothing happens by accident — not even the things that hurt us the most, unfortunately. If you lack the strength to find your way back to your heart and to process anger and frustration, life may lose its vibrancy and turn somber.

Your faithful dog companion signifies loyalty and unconditional love that transcend everything. He is here to remind you of this, and together, we will guide you on the right path. We love you, as does Heaven. Invest your energy on something important to you right now. Your worries and fears about the future come from a lack of confidence. Remember, life flows as long as you live it in every moment. It is up to you how you live it. Pay attention to the signs which are not mere coincidences — these are clear messages of support. Heaven always has a plan, but its grandeur can at times elude human comprehension. We swear or get angry until we don't believe in anything anymore. This is part of your healing process. But at some point, this energy must be transformed, otherwise it will hurt you. Myself, the dog spirit, and Heaven are here to help you — we are here for you.

Carry or sleep with me as long as you want; we will give relief to your heart. Write your thoughts down. It is not important what or how you write, but your intention to transform your inner pain is. When you wish, wash me under water and expose me to sunlight so that I can recharge myself.

We hope that life offers you the chance to be awed by the path ahead, rekindling your trust in life itself. May you also realize, dear soul, the depth of love and support surrounding you, evident in the messages and serendipities you encounter in various forms each day.

AMETHYST

To go beyond appearance, open yourself to a new vision.

DEAR SOUL, WELCOME! I AM THE AMETHYST, A FORTRESS of information with immense imaginative and creative power. Yes, I create! I create what you think, what you dream, and what you cannot imagine, by going beyond what you see with your eyes.

Many roads lead to me, depending on the timing. I am always in motion like a swing. My energy is strong, ethereal, and sometimes intangible. I can be stubborn and dense. Not everyone can handle me because they never know what to expect. I can lead you to explore infinite worlds and dimensions, but also make you touch your darkest, fixed thoughts and limiting beliefs.

I come to you because you are getting lost inside your thoughts, which create fear and confusion. They don't help you see the truth — on the contrary, they bring you fatigue and restless sleep. When this happens, don't get caught up in your thoughts — watch them pass as if they were clouds in the sky. We often think we are our thoughts, but we are not.

Work with me and call forth a power that connects you to the creative universe. Don't get lost in fluctuating and confusing thoughts. You need a change of perspective. Calm your mind, and unveil a new vision beyond the realm of ordinary sight. Follow the little luminous spirits of the cricket, ancient voices whispering from the unseen world, leading you to the front door of your mind. There you can truly connect to something sacred, and see everything with the eyes of spirit, trusting what you are observing.

Magic and alchemy are part of me, and together we can help you find your answers — although you will realize that not all answers are attainable. But when you do, you will see that sometimes it is not so important to have them. However, there is a precious treasure chest in your mind which must be in service to your heart, going beyond personal ego. Do you understand now how important it is that you clean your mind?

Work from the center of your heart to the center of your mind and connect the two. There you will be able to see the stars. Great opportunities await you, but always remember that within every weakness resides an inherent strength. Help yourself with meditation and visualization exercises, or even with dancing or cooking. Find a way to give your mind a rest.
If you want, you can take me with you at any time — I will help you gain clarity, protect you from outside influences, and amplify your talents. Just as you need to clean your mind, I—being out of my natural environment—need to recharge. Wash me under water and expose me to the moonlight, crescent or full, whenever you feel the desire to do so.

We hope you find surprise in the way your mind can effortlessly become light, creative, and radiant in service to your heart.

ANGELITE

Find the balance necessary to be an angel on Earth.

DEAR SOUL, WELCOME. I AM THE ANGELITE SPIRIT, and my name evokes a very strong image and status. I arrive with my wise owl companion to remind you that your talents are abundant and diverse, offering both opportunities and challenges. We serve as messengers to remind you of your true self and the responsibilities you bear as a soul in your earthly journey. While we ask you to be an angel on Earth, right now you are becoming too immersed in the role, bringing home others' problems as if they were your own. This does not benefit you or the people around you.

By nature, you are a listening soul, so you would be inclined to be a therapist or a leader in service to your community — people are naturally drawn to you for advice. But you need to know one important thing. Owl and I do not help unless we are asked. We don't solve problems for someone else. To be an angel on Earth means to support, to stand by, and eventually guide in the direction in which you need to turn your gaze. This is the true helping relationship; in love there is no other way. Conversely, too much help can be addictive. In order to grow—or help others to grow—you have to allow them the freedom to make mistakes while standing by their side.

I trust this is clear enough for you. If not, ask yourself — what resistances are clouding your view?

Assisting others to become emotionally free and independent is noble work and a precious gift. I am here to help you through a subtle, yet effective communication aligned with a higher good. Now, practice detachment with love in various situations. Look at everything with different eyes — like an owl can turn her head 360 degrees. Look at things from multiple viewpoints and wonder what is the highest good for all. Put these talents of yours into practice, and don't take on others' problems at the cost of your own wellbeing.

We stand by you and support you. If you want to take me with you, I will be with you everywhere — whether you're asleep or awake, at work or at play. I love to be exposed to lunar energy, rising or full. Wash me lightly under water because I am delicate.

Your soul and person can leave a big mark on the world. When you follow our suggestions, you will realize how rewarding it is for everyone. Being an angel on Earth is such a great love that you will only realize it by experiencing it. We hope you align with what your talents demand, allowing your service to transform into a true gift.

APOPHYLLITE

Let your soul fly from the conditioning of others.

I AM THE SPIRIT OF APOPHYLLITE, AND IT IS WITH great pleasure that I welcome you today. You must know, dear soul, that my energy comes from above the heavens. I have different shades, and my radiance gives instant tranquility simply by gazing at me. I seem to come from another planet, and that is indeed the case.

I bring with me beautiful sacred dragonflies, bearing gifts of fresh ideas, serenity, and lightheartedness, all while infusing depth into your soul. Our iridescence transports you to the center of the universe where everything is perfect as it is. In that place, nuances make a difference. Dear soul, you should adopt this perspective as well, enabling you to integrate these nuances into your life.

While a luminous soul lives within you, your thoughts can sometimes become confused. Your breathing becomes labored, and you feel like everything escapes you. The aspects of yourself that manifest your desires are those that yearn for control over situations, inhibiting the natural flow of things in their entirety. By doing so, do you recognize that you cannot have a clear perspective of what is transpiring within you and around you? Life is like the constant to-and-fro of a swing, teaching you how results occur based on your choices. Like on a swing, someone else pushes you, you can swing yourself, or you can stand still. But how nice it is to sway suspended in the air like a dragonfly! You need to develop the mindset of being open to the possibility of new experiences and taking risks without a fearful 'it can't be done' attitude. When the universe came into being, it had no definite plan to follow, simply the sense that it needed to explode with the intention to create and let things manifest spontaneously. You are a fragment of the universe; you must not forget that. Venture beyond dimensions and raise your spiritual level — there you will find the light and a deep inner joy.

In your everyday life, take a moment to consider which parts you can nurture to fly higher and enjoy the journey. Dare to push yourself harder on the swing and bring out your impulsiveness. You are here on Earth to experience as much of a joyful life as possible. Face your problems today with a different attitude and be mindful of what I have shared. Re-evaluate everything, and you will notice how your vision changes and takes on fresh significance.

I can be very helpful to you when you meditate or visualize. Center yourself and breathe, make your mind as calm as possible, and express a clear intention of where you want me to take you to explore — otherwise you will find yourself in confusion. If you want to keep me in the house, let me rest in the bedroom, study room, or living room. I will help you raise the energy level of that environment so that you can benefit from it. I am a delicate stone, so wash me lightly with water when you feel it is appropriate and expose me to the light of the moon — new, crescent, or full.

We hope you find joy in your journey and maintain a conscious lightness when facing life's inevitable ups and downs. Always remember that you are an integral part of the universe.

AVENTURINE

Go back to laughing and playing in your life.

WELCOME DEAR SOUL, HERE I AM, HERE I AM! LOOK at me, don't I make you smile? Oh yes, I am the spirit of aventurine and I come to give you this message — breathe, smile, then smile again … and again … Hahaha!

No, I am not joking. I am coming along with my dear and wise turtle friend to tell you that you need to change your attitude toward life. You worry too much about what will happen in what you call 'the future'. You are approaching your relationships too seriously and with a strong sense of attachment. Your expectations are high, and as a result, it is inevitable you will be disappointed. Rediscover the art of letting go, releasing the fear of losing someone and relinquishing the need for control. The future holds many possibilities, and within you is a child eager to play in this life. They relate authentically, their heart knows no assumptions, and sees only what is there. They live to the fullest, rejoicing in the simplest of pleasures.

My turtle and I will help you breathe, lighten your heart, and remind you how to play to loosen your body from too much tension. Afterward, you will learn how to slow down and enjoy the essential little things.

Children are great teachers, so model your behaviors after them. Take yourself less seriously and laugh at yourself. When you do this and concern yourself with situations that seem heavy for you, you will notice how much lighter they seem.

Take me with you wherever you want, and I will help you lighten your mood. Immerse yourself in this card to smile again. When you feel I need a recharge, wash me and expose me to sunlight.

May your current moments be as delightful as that first experience of walking barefoot on grass, with its irresistible tickling sensation.

BLACK TOURMALINE

Protect your life field, guard and recover your energy.

DEAR SOUL, HOW TIRED, FATIGUED, AND BURDENED are you? I am here to tell you that you are not solely responsible for this. Now, however, is the time to take matters into your own hands. I am the spirit of black tourmaline who with strength, fierceness, and physical presence urges you to place boundaries around your living space.

You should be aware that your daily experiences and the individuals you interact with have a constant resonance in your life. If you allow events to engulf you without maintaining the necessary detachment, your innate energy can be compromised.

Your physical, emotional, and psychological stability can be affected to the point you find it hard to recognize yourself in your reactions. It is also true that all this arises throughout life to train your primary strength. Don't feel sorry for yourself or blame others. Simply take note of the situation and go from there to make things better.

Dear soul, if you allow yourself to be influenced by the energies and opinions of others, you may struggle to attain clarity, lucidity, a healthy emotional state, and the freedom to act in your life. Souls are vibrations, sounds, and energies constantly moving and interacting with your external world. The health status of your physical body is very important in this process, so requires healthy eating and activity to maintain the human vessel.

Our sacred lion friend, with his presence and pride, reminds you how important your sacred living territory is, including your home, work, and the places you frequent. Invasions or intrusions without consent are not allowed. He is ready to make his voice heard in times of need, either to bring the pack to attention or to retreat alone. He does so without justification, but with great presence and awareness.

Carry me with you during the day and I will restore your vigor. In places where you need it, I will help protect your living space. I advise you to take baths with rock salt to cleanse yourself deeply and cleanse your space with incense. Keep your chin up and take one step at a time. Take hold of your strength again. A great act of awareness is required of you for there to be a breakthrough. To keep me clean, wash me in water and expose me to sunlight so that I may recharge.

We wish for you to embrace life as an opportunity to strengthen your resolve and never underestimate the power of your own voice. It is your right and your duty to yourself.

BLUE CHALCEDONY

Let your dreams be your unconscious talking to you.

WELCOME, SWEET SOUL, I AM THE SPIRIT OF THE BLUE chalcedony. I live where time stands still, where dreams seem like reality, and where words remain unspoken verbally but expressed by the language of silence.

I dreamed that you needed me and my wise horse to calm your anger and frustration, granting you the capacity to communicate peacefully as needed. Before getting angry, take heed — if you wish to go to a higher level of your growth, know that profound inner work lies ahead, and you will have to position yourself to accomplish it. Furthermore, the horse is here to bestow upon you the serenity of pausing to savor the present moment. We can help restore your contact with nature and your surroundings. Open your eyes and look at the blue sky. Feel the breeze caress your face, and sense how you feel. The situations you are encountering will take on greater significance, but you will be able to address them in a more constructive manner.

You are precious, dear soul; your sensitivity is special. You are still not aware of what your potential is. It is for this reason we are here for you. Nurture within yourself the aspiration to evolve as a person and a spirit — you might even enjoy doing so. Given these qualities, you would make a good teacher, therapist, or any public-speaking figure, leaving a lasting mark with your words.

Reassure your soul, trust yourself, and restore your gaze to the beauty of life. It doesn't have to be all battle or toil — otherwise how will you dream, listen, or achieve your goals? Sleep is very important, because your deep sensitivity to the messages you receive at this time informs you about people and situations. I advise you to keep a notebook by your bedside to write down what you dream. You might surprise yourself.

Hold me close to your lungs and throat, and I will help you breathe by nourishing you. I will also aid you to truly listen. Keeping me in your home will bring beauty and harmony.

When you meditate with me, hold a flower in your hand and I will let you talk to it. I will work hard, so remember to recharge and cleanse me occasionally with water. Then expose me to the moonlight, crescent or full.

We hope you leave a remarkable trail filled with beauty and all that you aspire to become.

BLUE–GREEN LABRADORITE

Don't be afraid of who you are in the depth of your shadows — embrace them.

WELCOME DEAR SOUL, I AM THE SPIRIT OF LABRADORITE, and alchemy is one of my gifts. I look dark, but within me lies a rainbow. A sensual charm accompanies me, and I touch chords you cannot imagine.

It is now time to remove your emotional illusions. Look within, into the depths of your inner cave, where everything is hidden. Like a mirror in the shadows, you need to find your true power again. You're using this magical place as a hideout, employing a myriad of excuses out of fear of uncovering your true self. Within you exist the eyes of a seer, peering beyond the folds of your personality and tapping into the great wisdom of time. Whoever you have been in your various lives, dear soul — now is the time to remember and bring them to fruition.

I come to you with my sacred friend bear. We gaze straight into your eyes and bring you into our depths. Do you want to see the truth or not? Do you want this mirror we bring you as a gift to be your ally or your enemy? At times, you conceal yourself, avoiding the sight of your own depth, which can evoke feelings of loneliness, helplessness, and sadness. Yet do you not recognize the profound depths within you?

Magic and science merged in ancient times into an alchemical solution. We want you to know that the true magic, awakened by a precious soul, only emerges after it has journeyed through its darkest depths. This process can sometimes be almost bloody, but it inevitably leads the soul to transform its shadows into light. All of this guides it toward a higher level of consciousness, where it can truly work magic, much like the unexpected reflections the sacred moon casts on a serene lake.

We have come to you because we can support you. Remove the veils and connect to that feeling; take time and work on it. My advice is to look for the truth in what is in front of you, then ask yourself if it is consistent with your feelings. Embrace bear and feel how much power resides in them. They can be extremely gentle, protective and friendly, but also fierce and quick when they have to act.

When you carry me with you, I will help you make your cave a gift. Meditate with me and I will lead you to unexpected depths. I am connected to the moon, so expose me to her when you feel that I need to catch my breath and return to my full strength.
We hope you discover in your lifetime the beauty you see in the mirror and the depth of sensitivity and wisdom you can offer each day.

BOTSWANA AGATE

Find your way back into your deepest desires.

IF YOU FIND YOURSELF IN A TIME OF CONFUSION, THE events that have happened to you have led you astray because you wanted to follow someone else's needs. Look at me. Focus, observe me, and delve into me. I will guide you into the depths of yourself. I am the spirit of the Botswana agate. A proud warrior, I give you my support. It will take time, but I will help you find your true nature and give you the opportunity to realize it in practical ways.

I am deep and probably difficult to understand, but I assure you that with patience and anticipation—just as in a time of gestation—I will help you bring forth a new vision within you. Your inner eye will be activated! Don't be afraid. By doing this you will call forth your power.

Wait before making a choice. Take your time and seek clarity. Assist your body in supporting you, which in turn will strengthen your energy field. The wonderful geckos are here to raise your energy and cool your fiery blood at this time. They are creatures who bring prosperity and confidence while teaching you patience. Become aware of your state and allow these guides to empower you in finding the path you feel resonates the most.

Enter the deep waters of your being so a new sensuality and procreative force can manifest. Cleanse yourself using the water element — take restorative baths and drink plenty of water. Meditate with me, and I will guide you into yourself. Inhale new energy, and you will find yourself centered and strong.

We hope your journey brings you a continuous sense of renewal. Remember — the beauty in your everyday experiences gives you the opportunity to rediscover yourself in constant movement, just as life is.

CARNELIAN

Have fun singing and dancing to honor your life.

WELCOME, DEAR SOUL. TODAY, I INVOKE THIS MOMENT for you. I am the spirit of the carnelian, and the rhythm of life resides within me. I approach you like a dance, propelled by the beat of a drum, chasing butterflies. Everything beckons you to release and free yourself from emotional rigidity. Life is in constant motion, and attempting to control it contradicts its very nature. With joy and a smile, I encourage you to relinquish control. Your profound cosmic waters—your emotions—which are a source of strength, have been compressed.

Be creative, be crazy, and be irreverent. Step away from rigid patterns that dictate 'how things should be done', including those imposed by external expectations. You've confined yourself with guilt and the division between what's considered right and wrong. However, you must come to realize that you cannot imprison a free, liquid-like essence. This only complicates your life. Dance as lightly as a butterfly of a thousand shades of color. They are not beautiful or ugly, but they have a special beauty in their uniqueness. In my world, there exists no fixed mindset that dictates a single way of doing things. Instead, it's a realm where all that brings you happiness is embraced, and you have the freedom to pursue them in a manner that aligns with your desires and the greater good of all.

We will be happy to accompany you in this transformation. Maybe it's time to sign up for a dance class or a creative workshop of some kind. Perhaps you want to move furniture around the house, or paint a wall a bold, new color. I am an inspiration to artists, madmen and anarchists. An ancient magic resides in your belly, where the art of listening ascends to a higher plane, but only if it is granted the freedom to express itself freely. Practice self-observation and pay attention to your interactions with others. Notice how frequently you seek to control situations. Then, with small yet profound steps, initiate the transformation where it's necessary.

If you wish, wear me during the day, and I will help you be creative. Together, we will make sure we dance. When you feel I need it, wash me under the water and expose me to sunlight. We hope that life will astonish you with your own beauty as you dance with the very essence of life, filled with joy.

CELESTINE

Embrace with a light smile the passages of life.

I AM THE SPIRIT OF THE CELESTINE. MY COLOR IS reminiscent of heavenly light, which I am powerfully connected with. I can listen to birds and understand them, and I can hear the songs and messages of angels. The trees and the wind tell me their stories. Ethereal beauty resides in me.

I can work with you in many ways and on many levels because I carry luminous thoughts and faith in the existence of the great Heavenly Father. If you are accompanying a soul to ascension—whether human or animal—entrust them to me. I will support them like a gentle caress. I bring consolation, compassion, and soothe the wounds of loss, and I can help you see the bigger picture. When I am with you, you will feel the deep love of Heaven within you anew, as if you were experiencing it as a child for the first time.

Let go of your inflexibilities and anger, because life is not always the way you want it to be. Embrace the love that exists even when you can't perceive it at this moment. Your connection would be strong if not for the fact that your mind is currently preoccupied with many superfluous matters. The light, singing birds in this image are here, with me, to remind you what it means to hold a sense of wonder. Allow yourself to continue to be amazed and able to see the deep beauty in all you experience. Nourish yourself with the love, tenderness, and kindness that you feel when you hold a little bird in your hands.

When you look at this card or hold a piece of celestine in your hand, a sweet smile will rise on your face. You will realize that all the thoughts crowding your mind are useless. The distinct feeling that there is something bigger than you will emerge, and you will feel small in the face of it. With me by your side, you will be able to sleep peacefully. If you meditate, I will take you to distant, bright places. Wear me on your person, and I will lighten your mood. Keep me in your home, and I will make it harmonious.

When you feel the need, wash me lightly under water and expose me to moonlight, crescent or full. Remember well what I have said because a sensitive and kind heart lives in you and should not be neglected.

We hope, dear soul, that throughout your life, you may feel a profound sense of belonging to something greater, filling your being with radiant thoughts.

CHRYSOCOLLA

Create your own world inspired by beauty.

DEAR SOUL WHO COMES TO ME, I INTRODUCE MYSELF. I am the spirit of chrysocolla. Green and blue are my shades, and the oceans and earth merge as our beloved Gaia. I am the lush earth, I give beauty and abundance, and the spirits of Earth and Heaven create through me.

It is time to bring your thoughts and emotions to a higher vibrational level so you can manifest your deepest desires. Yes, you now have the opportunity to fearlessly release all that is barren within you. You have lost confidence over time because of past events. You must remember, dear soul, that Mother

Earth suffers if it does not rain for a long time, or if her oceans, seas, and rivers remain polluted. Think of them as her emotions, perpetually needing to flow to nourish her. She cannot allow life on her to dry up and, in fact, has put in place a cycle that harmonizes the whole ecosystem. I am communicating this to you because you are losing yourself behind a thousand excuses. You are polluting your being, resisting change and the desires within you that need to be expressed. By doing so, you fail to see beauty where it is — and I assure you, dear soul, that beauty is everywhere, even where you think it is not.

Fly like the wonderful flying rays that approach you. They weren't born to fly, but when enthusiasm takes over, they take a leap high above the surface of the water. Their beauty is unique and may not be seen by some people's eyes. This is their message to you — "Enthusiasm is a divine quality that attracts everything to you and makes great things happen." When you cultivate this quality within the depths of your emotions, it becomes a tale worth telling. This is our advice to you. We are connected because you are a child of Heaven and Earth. I am in your belly, in your womb, in your heart, and in your thoughts. You can't let the fear of failure hold you back any longer. It is time for you to begin a new adventure that resonates with your inherent beauty. Heaven and Earth will always support you. You are a soul born in the world and for the world. Live this life to the fullest, or you'll be left with only regrets.

Carry me around as much as you want, and I will help you see the beauty in yourself and in the art of creating. When you meditate with me, you can connect to the spirit that unites everything. When you see fit, wash me under flowing water and expose me to the light of the sun, but it's best to keep me out of direct sun, or you can choose lunar light, crescent or full.

We wish for your life to be filled with enthusiasm for the beauty of your true self, acknowledging it fully.

CITRINE QUARTZ

Be a balanced and strong, self-aware fire.

I AM THE SPIRIT OF CITRINE QUARTZ AND I COME to help you listen and feel your inner fire. I will lead you to the 'I Am' affirmation, which you should learn to observe with detachment and respect. This way, it won't be your ego dominating, but your innate fire. You may not trust yourself today, dear soul, but know that the whole universe is rooting for you. You have within you a great gift of fire, but it needs to be trained and managed, so that it does not backfire on you.

Sometimes you shut down out of fear because you sense an anger that you cannot handle! You may feel you are not up to the task of being able to make your own contribution to life, or at other times you are so exuberant that you provoke others so much and generate chaos. Stop now! Your stomach and liver are clamoring for attention. You need to rebalance your life energy. Visualize a flame in the center of your body, rising from your navel to your chest, bring it back to its natural state. Breathe into it and calm that excess heat.

From the majestic earth to the tree of knowledge that dwells within you, the sacred and watchful hawk looks down on you to help you in your life choices — who you want to be and what you wish to manifest. The fire, the hawk, and I invite you to transform your anger and your resentment. It is your ego that feels this way, but it is only a part of you. Download all the excess to the great Mother Earth, she will sustain you. Throw these emotions into the fire and turn them into grit and self-confidence so you can find your true spark. Whenever you have to make a choice or make a decision, rely on this spark. Listen to how you feel in a given situation and then act as the hawk does — proud and confident, aware of their power, and what they are doing. The result may not be the most crucial aspect; instead, it's self-awareness in carrying out the necessary actions that matters.

If you want to take me with you, I will support you during the day because I love the sun. I am very responsive, so keep me as long as you see fit. You can meditate with me whenever you want to contact your divine spark. When you feel the need, wash me under water and expose me to sunlight.

We hope that your inner fire will continue to radiate, lighting your path with purposeful and mindful deeds.

GARNET

Embrace the honor-filled warrior in you.

IN EARTHLY LIFE YOU CANNOT ALWAYS BE MEEK. IF YOU want to actualize your dreams, you have to stop feeling like a victim of a fate you don't like. This is your test. As the spirit of garnet, my help can be crucial to you — with me, there are no more excuses, only actions.

You may be feeling at a standstill or that your energy is stuck. You need to take back your life. I will help coach you, and together with the cheetah, we are here to awaken your inner warrior and your self-confidence, and to get your vital and creative energies going again.

In many ancient legends, the spirit of the warrior invoked love, respect, boldness, and honor — not in the absence of fear, but rather, by embracing it. The cheetah is here to teach you how to develop a strategy that leads to action. Free yourself from your past, marked by the belief that, "It will always go wrong, I will struggle, and achieve nothing in the end." Reconnect with this age-old truth — "The hunter who is in need and seeks his prey with respect and tenacity will always find it." Be strong within, for we stand with you, and together we can achieve anything.

Remember, dear soul, you can do anything, but only if you really want it. Otherwise, you will blindfold yourself with excuses and justifications, or you will find yourself always blaming your defeats on someone else. In this way, it will certainly be inevitable that you will remain as meek as a lamb. It is always a matter of choice.

If you want to take me along, I will strongly support you. You should know that I love to be worn during the day. If you want to meditate or travel with me, I will help you recognize your blocks. When you feel the need to recharge, wash me under running water and expose me to sunlight.

Believe in what you can accomplish. We believe in you, and we trust life will affirm your belief in yourself.

HEMATITE

Let your blood be renewed to bestow new strength.

DEAR SOUL, YOU ARE TIRED, I KNOW. YOUR LEGS ARE heavy, and you probably have people near you who cannot be called light of heart or thought. I am the spirit of hematite — and yes, I am tough! You should know that one of my main components is iron. Within my veins flows the essence of life. Many people are scared at the sight of blood but there is nothing to fear, since it represents life.

The sacred crocodile is here to eat away all the heaviness of what you are experiencing — psychologically, emotionally, or physically. Toxic, limiting thoughts are bringing you down.

Your usual attitude cannot give you the boost you need now. It's time to raise your head and change your mindset. With the power of the sun and the earth, we are here to help you regain your strength, especially your physical strength. When you are iron-deficient, you may even suffer from deep sadness. We don't want that for you, instead we want you to regain your breath, enthusiasm, and will to live. Help yourself with good nutrition, take care of yourself, and if you can, detach yourself a little from situations so that you give yourself time.

Observe the strength that comes from this image — it's time to sharpen your teeth, and the crocodile has plenty of those! Let your blood be clean of all the dross you carry around that is not always yours. The energy of the earth nourishes you. I, hematite, will support you to recover your energy, and the crocodile will eat everything that no longer serves you. Together we can do this, but now it is up to you to decide and implement. A great emotional drive must arise in you. Life is a cycle — blood is renewed every day, giving us many possibilities to renew ourselves. Help yourself by changing what you need to and everything will return to as it should be.

You can carry me with you throughout the day, and I will support you during this time. I love the sun, so when I have done my work, wash me and lie me out in the sunshine to recharge and be ready for when you need me again.

We wish for your blood and life to be brimming with vitality so you can live life to the fullest.

HERKIMER

Ancient universal memories are awakening.

WELCOME, DEAR SOUL, I AM THE SPIRIT OF A VERY special and shining crystal — herkimer. Within me lives an ancient memory, where trees are sacred, waters are blessed, and the deva (nature spirits) are light workers. I am the fruit of an act of love between Father Sky and Mother Earth, which took place at the beginning of time. From their union was I born.

A sacred and ancient humpback whale accompanies us, her healing song taking us back to the dawn of time. She is the keeper of the memories of the crystals. Her gaze, full of compassion and gentleness, downsizes the ego of the human being, bestowing love and knowledge. Today we come to bless and serve you, so that you can shine the light of the soul within you and bring it into daily life.

You are a precious soul with a gift for connecting with subtle energies. Your task is to teach others about these, which will be easier if your connection to Mother Earth is strong. Work on your personal ego so that it does not affect the message you have to bring, regardless of your current or future practices. My crystalline grid is strong and always expanding. I can take you to other dimensions and places you may have only read about in fairy tales. Your mind must be empty, surrendered to your vision, otherwise everything may become more confusing. The folds of your soul are full of memories just waiting to be remembered, and we are here for that too.

This is a moment where these talents can be made available to others. Humility, heart, mind, and soul must be in clean connection with each other. If you have to make a choice in your life, listen to everything we are telling you. Root yourself into the ground — there you will find counsel. Meditation, seeking vision, and listening can be helpful to you at this time. If you wish to take me with you, know that I can be as close as you wish. I will facilitate your soul's manifestation. Meditate with me, and you will touch the brightest light within you. Being a clear, bright, clean, humble, and responsible soul is not easy, I know. But this is your nature.

We hope that life provides you with the chance to incorporate your soul's memories into your daily life, enabling you to offer them in service to humanity with deep gratitude.

HYALINE QUARTZ

You are a precious soul full of light.

I AM THE SPIRIT OF THE QUARTZ, THE ROCK CRYSTAL, representing the light of the soul and the vibrant water where all things melt and flow. Within me resides the energy that flows throughout your entire being, providing flexibility in navigating life's changes. Today we are gathered here for you, dear soul - to celebrate you.

As you can see in this card, multiple sacred animals are with me to honor your transition and the awareness of how much your soul needs care and nourishment. Although you have much to do, you have come from a time that was not easy, leaving you feeling confused. You are too precious to us for you to be lost. Stop for a moment, reflect on what is going on within and around you. Your physical and energetic presence is needed now — you cannot escape change. Life is movement, energy is in motion, as is everything. You cannot afford to stiffen in the face of it. If you keep throwing tantrums, your body will become rigid, along with your thoughts, and, I assure you, that is not good.

The same potential inherent in quartz crystal lives within you. It's evident that, to harness this ability, life will present you with situations aimed at helping you break and dissolve established patterns. Life loves you, remember that. The element of water—flowing with vitality—cannot be tamed but ridden. Or you can decide to be rocked by it, surrendering to a state of full acceptance.

Pause before making decisions and take time to listen to where your soul wants to place yourself in this life. Let this energy flow through you, let it cleanse and break through the obstacles blocking your flow. Connect silently to the question, "What kind of light do I want to be in this world?" When the answer becomes clear to you, celebrate this wonderful moment with a feast.

Come visit us during your meditations, visualizations, or shamanic journeys. We will be there waiting to commune with you and give you rest. You will feel at home. You can take me with you wherever you want, in all my forms. I will support you during your personal work. If you feel I need a recharge, expose me to sunlight or moonlight after being washed. I also work well at home and in the workplace, protecting and bringing heavenly light into your environments.

We eagerly await your celebration and hope that you experience the beauty of being fully present with yourself and your soul in life, becoming a unique light in this world.

KYANITE

Beings of light have a message for you;
open yourself to receive it.

WELCOME, DEAR SOUL. I AM THE SPIRIT OF KYANITE— or 'disthen', or 'sapparite', whatever you want to call me—I am here for you today. The water, the sky, and the beings of light are with me. My color is an azure blue, one that only nature can paint. Great connections and great talents await us. So many things we can do together, if you wish. I have the strength and speed of a waterfall coming rushing down from the sky.

Did you know you are a unique soul? Why then do you feel your nature weighs you down? Today, I bring with me two magnificent white horses to convey the depth of pride, beauty, and purity that emanates from your inner self. Embrace it all and give us the opportunity to help expand your mind and vision so you can achieve otherworldly communication. You have no idea how many psychic levels there are and the joy and serenity you feel as you travel toward them. Do you feel your body's energy rising as you contemplate this wonder? We are conveying beautiful concepts that are hard to articulate, but we urge you to clear your mind, as this task is very important.

Receiving and projecting other people's energies is illusory. An unclean connection can lead you to dangerous choices and directions, which is why it is important that you continue to cleanse yourself and your space. Don't underestimate the toxicity you can pick up from others' thoughts — protect yourself. Release yourself from personal attachments as they will not set you free. This is the reason you feel you often have to isolate yourself. If you learn to manage these talents, you can live a more balanced life. Your intelligence allows for fast learning. Study, learn, and deepen your skills by putting them into practice. However, don't let theory and technicalities sabotage your empathy. Maintain an openness and curiosity to listening to yourself. When you need to rest your mind, immerse yourself in the beauty of this card's image and refresh yourself under the waterfall.

When you wear me, I will help you and remind you of all this. Put me under your pillow at night, and I will help you create powerful dreams. If you meditate or travel with me, you can contact and maybe communicate with beings of light or your essence. Wash me lightly under water and expose me to moonlight — new, rising, or full.

We hope that these talents, bestowed upon you from birth, are employed for the greater good of all, bringing you immense joy.

LAPIS LAZULI

Wisdom from the heart and healed ego
is manifested through the word.

WELCOME, DEAR SOUL, I AM THE SPIRIT OF LAPIS lazuli. My color is a deep blue with golden sparkles; great painters have used me to make their paintings celestial. I am a royal stone, communicating through the heart and expressing myself through the spirit. My presence is full of charisma, and I assure you it is felt.

Accompanying me today are beautiful white herons. We are here to tell you that it is time to make peace within yourself, it is time to put wisdom into your words and begin to manifest your countless gifts. The proud herons want to give you a sense of balance, stability, and the ability to discern between your energy and that of others. It is not always easy to be present with yourself and consistent with what you manifest in deeds and words. And, dear soul, you often find an excuse to explain everything that occurs. Your potential is boundless. The teachings are already imprinted within you; all that's left is to reopen the pages of your memoir.

Given your many qualities, you could be a good leader or teacher. You can get your point across clearly, having great charisma. Or you could be a splendid creative, manifesting through the art of cooking or singing. Do you realize how much you can be? You just have to follow your passions. Consider training yourself using coaching methods or even get involved with theater. This would help you bring out that fluency you need, without fear. It is not about a constructed fluency though, but rather your natural expressiveness that will emerge.

When you have moments of confusion, remember another of your talents is writing. Use it to put all your thoughts in black and white. Your mind will calm, anger will transform, and you will become clear-headed again so you can communicate your thoughts without fear. There is a saying that states, "You are responsible for what you say, but not for what others understand!" At least, up to a point. You should be able to reach the point where communication is crystal clear and free of shadows of doubt on both sides. Do your best — this is your task.

I will be a great working tool for you while you carry me on your person. During rest I will protect your dreams. Placing me in your workspace will help improve communication between you and your colleagues. If you teach, I will be happy to stand on your desk. If you wish to meditate, I will take you to my palace. When you feel to, wash me under the water and expose me to solar energy.

We hope you enhance your charismatic presence, to benefit both yourself in your daily life and to serve others.

MALACHITE

Accomplish, celebrate, protect your greatest goals.

TODAY, THERE IS A GREAT CELEBRATION FOR YOU, A ceremony, a passage of life, an initiation — everything is ready. I am the spirit of malachite, and I bring new ideas, births, abundance, waiting, and patience for the fruits of the earth to be ripe for you.

My intense color, striped green, comes from primordial Mother Earth, where songs of women echo in the powerful air. Spread the news of something new to the world through the wind. Whether it's a project or a child, it holds an indescribable strength and love that emanates from the heart. I bring with me the familiar energy of those who stand by you and assist you in the highlights. If you need to nurture a situation or heal something physical within you, wearing me can help you where excess heat creates inflammation.

I am here today with my sacred and wise friends, the elephants, to support you in your life passage and to remind you that patience is a divine quality. Knowing how to wait for the right moment sometimes proves crucial to taking the right steps. Elephants have great legs to walk firmly on the earth and leave their indelible mark.

Everything is being prepared for you to achieve what you desire. We are with you to protect and support you. However, you must be very clear with yourself and not be in a hurry. Always remember that Heaven and Earth are looking forward to celebrating with you. Everything comes precisely when the time is ripe, neither before nor after. The moment of gestation must be understood and savored. Create, imagine, and feel it in your heart. This is the right way. We will support you.

I prefer to be worn alone, at least at first, to give you better support. Use me either during the day or at night, and just lean on me where you feel discomfort in your body, and I will soothe your pain. When you no longer feel the need for my support, wash me and expose me to the sun or moon, perhaps resting on the earth or on the pot of a plant.

We hope you continue to create, for your presence and contributions on Earth are needed.

MOONSTONE

Sister Moon's magic and teachings are your allies.

FROM THE NIGHT OF TIME, I ILLUMINATE AND CREATE night shadows. I am silence, observation, fullness, and cyclicity. I am the spirit of moonstone and I come to you to awaken your transformative power, creation, and deep magic.

In the natural cycle of growth, decline, and fullness—or whatever else you are experiencing in life—I am always there. I am connected to you, irrespective of gender, because I connect to your deep, sensitive, empathic, psychic, and primal essence. Like a serpent shedding their skin, I regenerate and become new periodically, connected to transformation. Now I invite you to do so — renew who you are.

The moon urges you to be still, observe what is in front of you and follow your intuition. Remember that the moon, while standing still, moves the tides. It is an apparent stillness, as it simply pushes and moves using its internal, conscious energy.

Stop stubbornly repeating the same situations over and over again. With each new cycle, you learn something new about yourself. Listen to the magic within you, become aware of the gift of empathy you possess, your way of listening, and how many messages come to you in night dreams — they will tell you a lot. Start with your nightly dreams or daily insights. Don't judge them, simply write them down. Read them and start asking yourself what they have to say. Clean out your ego-intoxicated emotions, and let go of what doesn't serve you, to make space for something new.

Together with the sacred, transformative serpents (who sometimes scare you), we invite you to enter into your sacred cosmic waters. Let your memories emerge and use our mutual sensitivity to make yourself who you are. Whether you are a sorcerer or a witch, a healer or a shaman, a doctor or a psychologist, use your talents in your daily life because you are needed.

Cleanse your physical body, especially your kidneys and intestines, with techniques that resonate most with you. Keep your hormones balanced to help you regulate mood swings.

Meditate with me by seeking that deep listening — I will guide you until I touch your sensitivity. Carry me whenever you want, and I will amplify your feeling. I love being washed and exposed to the light of the moon, crescent or full, when you feel it necessary.

We wish for you to experience true, deep transformation within yourself, discovering the sweetness residing in your soul and putting it to good use in your life.

MOSS AGATE

Small things become important.

I AM THE SPIRIT OF MOSS AGATE, AND MY COLOR HAS shades of dark green. Within me lives a whole world just like in the moss of the underbrush. I am here to teach you about emotional depth and valuing all the things in life that matter.

I live within the forest, representing all aspects of life. I inhabit that small, often overlooked space that serves as the source of all creation. My strength lies in the microcosm reflected in the macrocosm, just to give you an idea of how deep I am.

The ants bring you the gift of their hard-working and constant labor, which they are naturally inclined to do. They are small, but they're very important. With their sense of togetherness and strength, regardless of size, they remind you how important it is to be unique and precious in natural balance.

Dear soul, are you perhaps sad today? We are here to help you restore your true sense of worth and rekindle enthusiasm for your pursuits. Becoming lost in pleasing all the trees in the forest, you have forgotten about yourself. You represent that underground moss that settles the seeds and grows the trees around you. Therefore, I would say that you matter!

You must know that you nourish others, but you forget to nourish yourself. So much so that you neglect yourself physically — your gut weakens, and you feel tired as a result. Now is the time for you to take care of yourself, in body and spirit. Start saying 'no' where you can, without feeling guilty. Rest, drink plenty of water, and let your bodily sap cleanse. Regain your strength and go for a walk in the woods if you can. Breathe in their calm and regenerate yourself by observing the beauty you can only find there. When you feel better, ask yourself what is really important. Your inner answer will be your fresh start.

Renew yourself and be reborn stronger than before. Don't worry, we will help you with that. If you want, you can take me with you — I will support you and become a good friend.

If you meditate with me, I will guide you into your emotional depths. When you feel to, wash me under the water and expose me to the moonlight, crescent or full.

We hope that the seemingly small aspects of your life become indispensable to you, bringing joy through your daily creations.

OCEAN JASPER

Go beyond your limits by tapping
into your emotional strength.

WELCOME, DEAR SOUL, I INTRODUCE MYSELF TODAY to accompany you at this time of very profound emotional transition. I am the spirit of ocean jasper, and already my name tells you many things. I am the connection between the strength of the earth and the rushing memories of the ocean. It is often said that standing before the vastness of the ocean makes one feel small, yet simultaneously strong with the hope of realizing one's dreams.

I can be unpredictable, but I'm always full of life. This I want to convey to you today so that you can tap into your deepest desires and emotions — the ones you do not allow yourself to express for fear of failure or loss of control.

I am accompanied by a sacred octopus, and perhaps their presence evokes a certain effect within you. In your mind, you might associate them with something perilous, but I assure you they are here to tell you, "Our essence is not only in our blood and bones — it is also the adrenaline from our actions and the endorphins of our emotions that make us feel alive." The octopus meditates and plans what they needs to achieve. They patiently wait for the right moment, they don't give up, and know how to defend themselves with cunning. Use the talents of the octopus to achieve your dreams.

Dear soul, do not be afraid. Step by step you can navigate through the deepest, ancient waters of your inner world, and bring forth this beauty to the surface. So much life stirs within you, just as it does within us.

Spending time in the ocean water nourishes you and urges you to push yourself beyond your mental limits. Be impetuous and passionate about life — this is the essence of the ocean. If you dive into our depths, you can experience a silence you have never heard, but with a disarming fullness. Now work on yourself and experience.

When I am with you, I will support you throughout your normal daily routines. If you meditate with me, we will explore your emotional depths together. Know that I love to be washed with water and exposed to the sun when you feel I need a recharge. We hope for you to be brimming with life and a fervent motivation to explore the depths of your true desires.

PETRIFIED WOOD

Make your past your strength in daily life.

I AM THE SPIRIT OF PETRIFIED WOOD, AND I AM HERE to speak to you about your past, its importance, and how much wisdom it can bring. I represent the memory of the standing people, the great master trees living within me. I come from times far away where human memory cannot reach.

Dear soul, you should know that when you are born, you are given the opportunity to grow and resolve the various knots that have formed in past lives. Your memories come from Heaven and Earth. Inscribed in your DNA is that of your ancestors and family lineage. You can only imagine how much memory you actually have within you. Be aware of the baggage you carry, which you will have to open and sort through in the course of your life so you can evolve. Work deeply and patiently — after all, it took me millions of years to be who I am.

Dear soul, ask yourself, "What from my past keeps coming back? How can I act?" Life—the teacher of this path—presents you with various problems to solve. If you do not learn, the scenario will not change. The actors may change, but what you have to learn will not change until you are able to close all those situations that are repeated in succession like circles. After that you will be able to start again.

When you close the karmic circles—which are teachings, not punishments—great things happen within you. Often, this presents as the ability to recall talents we have in our memory, finding ourselves able to do things that we didn't know we could do before.

A wonderful, sacred mammoth walks with me. Their message to you: "Your future is always connected with your past. Until you make peace with it or honor it, it will come knocking again!" Connect with the strength of your sap family. Ancestors are important and can give you new visions. Your soul is old, and your feeling is strong. Give great importance to this, as you can now complete the karmic circles and move forward.

So dear soul, I have given you a lot of information to work with — now it is your turn!

When you carry me with you throughout the day, I will support you in your journey of recognizing your past. When the time seems right for you to recharge me, I ask you to wash me with water and expose me to sunlight.

We hope your memories awaken, that the wisdom of the trees flows within you, and that you enjoy its fruits.

RAINBOW FLUORITE

Your mind can create beyond all limits.

I AM THE SPIRIT OF RAINBOW FLUORITE, FASCINATING in my nuances. I bring vision through all your senses and, as a result, clarity and truth reside in me. What I do, dear soul, is complex to explain. I am layered and very fast in my movement.

I am sometimes called 'She who transcends the confines of the limiting and conditioned mind'. I can amplify your senses to help you find solutions you would never think of, like a genius who solves, invents, and reaches where others do not. In addition, I can assist you with your studies and exam preparation. Now I'm here to help you regain mental clarity, as the fast pace has become disorienting and is distracting you from your focus. All of this creates a distorted reality where you can easily manipulate yourself.

Meet the sacred hummingbird, who brings curiosity and the knowledge of speed and precision. They know where to go, their ethereal magic is beautiful. They signify the diversity of multifaceted perspectives. Do you know how many things you could perceive just by giving yourself a chance to channel this energy? By cleansing your mind of other people's conditioning and beliefs, you will find your own truth and insights without being influenced.

A great talent resides within you, and this demands cleanliness, awareness, and clarity. You can be whoever you want to be in your human existence, so much so your abilities can be diverse and eclectic, a bit like all the colors of the rainbow.

Now release and make space. It helps to be surrounded by nature and animals because they know instinctively how to be calm, slow down, and listen. Carry me wherever and whenever you want, for as long as you need me. When you meditate with me and embrace the graceful flight of the hummingbird, we can journey to the place where the rainbow bridge exists, offering a myriad of possibilities. Wash me when necessary and expose me to the energy of the new, crescent, or full moon.

Dear soul, we can guide you upward, like a sage perched on a mountain — seeing all, yet detached. We hope life allows you to harness this potential with great wisdom.

RED JASPER

Fulfill and create beyond your fear of failure.

I AM NOT A STONE THAT CARESSES. I AM THE SPIRIT OF red jasper and I represent strength, tenacity, and combativeness. I come to help you tangibly achieve your goals. The sun and the earth rejoice before the souls who know how to build despite fear. It is time.

Yes, I am talking about creating, working to achieve something you materially desire. To do this, you have to put aside all your doubts. Your blood—the sap of life—must circulate strongly in you. Your legs—your roots—can feed on the energy of Mother

Earth. She provides support and creative inspiration, as she wants the best for you.

Summon the will, perseverance, confidence, and courage to pursue your desire. Whether you want to build a house, change your job, change your diet, or chase a dream, it is time for you to work on yourself steadily and get in touch with your desires. Perhaps it is time to think that the word 'impossible' is just a limitation of the mind. You do not lack ingenuity, so find your own solutions — laziness and excuses are your enemy. Observe Mother Earth — she creates every day and is never afraid to fail.

My friends the squirrels have come to remind you that, like them, you must always be prepared and cunning and make a plan. Even when obstacles arise—and they will—maintain your confidence and the tenacity to carry on. Open the door to Earth's energy and connect with her. We are born in Heaven, but we are fulfilled on Earth — never forget that.

So many aspects, including parenting, correspond with my essence. I am a very deep stone. I can help you soothe the wounds of abandonment and betrayal that have left you feeling unfulfilled and doubting your ability to reap rewards. We support you, so have faith in yourself. Carry me with you throughout the day, especially while working. When you feel I need it, wash me under water and expose me to sunlight.

We hope that life provides you with ample opportunities for material realization and abundant rewards.

RHODONITE

Even the greatest sorrows can become valuable allies.

WELCOME DEAR SOUL, I KNOW YOU HAVE TRAVELED A very long path. Many lives speak of you, and many trials and pains you have had to overcome. I understand well what you feel and what you experience.

I am the rhodonite spirit, a proud warrior with a deep heart who knows what forgiveness is and who knows every mark on your heart. My traveling companion is the sacred and ancient white bison, whose characteristics are sacrifice and gift. Oh yes, there is no self-respecting warrior who has not sacrificed for the benefit of someone else, who has not wounded themselves, leaving a permanent mark. You are just that, dear soul, and the white bison is here to honor the warrior in you and the wounds that reside in your heart. They are a legendary and wise animal, and they show themselves to you now.

It is time to do the deep healing you have been waiting for. You must make that wound become a scar full of strength, an indelible tattoo that reminds you of where you have come from. Leave aside being a victim of your pain. Now you can bow down and caress the bison, hold tightly within you the feeling of peace that springs forth, honor this healing and feel how deep and real it is. Free your soul, because it has a strength that even you cannot imagine.

Do not be afraid to love out of fear of being hurt, abandoned, or betrayed. Just love, because your heart and soul are here for that. If you free yourself from attachment, from possession, no one can hurt you anymore. It is your personality that is hurting, your soul knows it is time to let go so you can be free. I know that a soul like you understands what I am communicating to you. Whatever you are experiencing now, ask yourself how much it is affected by these wounds, observe yourself and ask yourself if you are acting as love would or as fear would.

I can be heavy or light, depending on how much will you have to heal and whether it is the right time to do it. Give yourself time because this healing cannot happen quickly. Take me with you, sleep with me, you can sing your pain but also your redemption, and I will support you.

Hold me for as long as you feel the need, and when you realize I need to be recharged, you can wash me under the water and expose me to the moonlight. In your heart and mind, recall the white bison; their strength will sustain you in accepting these wounds.

May your life be filled with experiences that reveal the love and wisdom within your heart.

ROSE QUARTZ

Everything can blossom in love.

WHEN YOU STAND BEFORE ME, YOU STAND IN YOUR holy grail. Unlike the mythical chalice made of gold and gems, however, I am unassuming, readily found, and often overlooked. That is why I am the most precious heart. I have no judgments and no resentments. I love with great depth. I know where the roots of my love are and where my gaze is turned. Humility, listening, and patience reside within me. You know, the heart is the engine of everything and is united with the universal heart.

Your inner garden resides in the heart. It is up to you whether you love it and make it an earthly paradise or a dumping ground of grudges, frustrations, and non-acceptance of who you are. Your ability to love profoundly is rooted in the depth of self-love, dear soul.

A white dove flies with me and is here to bring you calm. You know that you are loved, no matter what you do. You do not have to earn love or beg for it. Fly, heart ... fly beyond the beliefs of others. Fly free as your soul, who knows that everything is perfect as it is. You choose everything in your earthly life to experience the existence of love. If you did not schedule painful experiences for yourself, you could not enact this experience. The purpose of life itself is to love.

Don't go into victim mode. Focus on your heart and ask yourself the right questions. Only you can work on yourself and recognize your truth. When you act, for whom do you really do it? Are you doing it for others or because you lack something yourself? Are you seeking validation and recognition? Ask yourself these questions and even if you don't find your answers right away, take the first step. Trust in the wisdom of your heart. Human beings, in order to feel loved, are able to enact many relational dynamics. Be an observer of yourself and gently watch where you fall.

I will help with your self-esteem while you carry me on your person. If you want to calm your breathing and anxiety, breathe with me and feel my embrace. When you realize I need to recharge, wash me under the water and expose me to moonlight, crescent or full.

Our friend dove and I send our blessings and wish that life grants you the opportunity to embrace love in all its dimensions.

RUTILATED QUARTZ

Wisdom comes from life lessons
experienced on the skin.

HOW EXTRAORDINARY LIFE IS! WITH THIS PHRASE I want to welcome you today, dear soul. I am the spirit of rutilated quartz (or maidenhair) and within me are golden hairs that resemble those of angels. I carry the energy of transformation, humble yet ever-present, elevating energy through wisdom.

Every day, life presents you with the chance to understand your true self, even though you might choose to remain stationary because you lack the determination to bravely examine what is amiss. Taking responsibility for your actions is not for everyone. It means being present to yourself and being humble enough to seek help when you need it.

A significant journey of change has led you to me, with the purpose of assisting you in organizing your thoughts and restoring your strength. I bring you this gift: a medicine bag. I want to offer you this tool so that you can turn your personal baggage into a gift. Inside you will find strength, confidence, courage, and acceptance.

A fox is here with us to remind you of the beauty of the path you have traveled so far, the lessons you've acquired, and the things you've left in your wake. In moments of need, avoid reverting to old patterns of the mind. If you desire, you can transform, dear soul. Avoid relying on anger or egoic impulses. Instead, use your emotional intelligence, which has grown wise. Use it and listen to it. Let me be clear, however — this does not mean be passive.

When the time is ripe, wisdom will make your worldview change. Your mind will be calmer, and your heart will no longer have the need to fill its own gaps. You will no longer want to overrule someone or change their mind. You will no longer feel the need to prove yourself. What will come will be the need to take a good, liberating breath, perhaps followed by a smile. The truly wise person knows how to laugh very well at themself. We are here to accompany you and remind you of all this.

Listen to yourself, breathe in your new, evolved energy. You certainly should not think you have it all figured out because otherwise you will fall off quickly, and that is typical of being human. We urge you to connect to that force of the spirit that is in union with the heart, now that spark has ignited. If you fall, you will get back up quickly because you will be aware that you have learned something else.

When you hold me on your person during the day, you won't lose touch with your spark. I love to be washed and exposed to the sun when you see fit. When you meditate with me, I will guide you to meet the wise spirit that resides within you, who laughs and already knows everything.

We hope that in this lifetime, you get to savor the freedom that washes over you when mental patterns shatter, and that you harness the thundering voice of your spirit by utilizing all the tools at your disposal.

SAPPHIRE

Be true to yourself by accepting the
splendor of your soul.

WELCOME, DEAR SOUL, I HEAR YOU AND SEE YOU FOR who you really are. These are some of my talents, and today more than ever you need me. I am the sapphire spirit; my color is a very distinctive indigo blue. My communication is more vibrational than verbal. I can understand and listen to those in front of me on a deeper level. These are qualities that resonate with you and belong to you, but that you are forgetting to use right now.

I am here with my sacred friend, Fawn, who invokes delicacy, innocence, and intense magic to connect you to the purity of spirit. We can lead you to your original source to re-contact these qualities that are indispensable for you now. Can you say that you are true to yourself at this time in your life? How much do you try to please others to make them like you or not judge you in your choices? Listen to yourself and breathe deeply. How do you feel today? Yes, you can give yourself permission to unite your personal part with the desires of spirit, without having the fear of being alone. Stay where you are by being yourself. True magic could happen at this level.

Dear soul, you are a person who can help others in many ways, even if only by example (probably the hardest part) because of the vibrations you have, but you must commit yourself to dissolving the old beliefs you have built up. Love yourself more and respect yourself for who you are — you can always improve.

Look at this wonderful card and sense what emotions are triggered within you. Breathe into them. When you meditate with me, I will take you to that magical place where there is presence of self, where no storm can shake you because you will be firm and strong. If you wear me, I will help you consistently communicate in alignment with your true nature. Wash me with water and expose me to moonlight, crescent or full. If you want me to shed any rigidity I've absorbed from you, place me in the light of the waning moon.

We wish for you to discover the presence within yourself in your everyday life, allowing you to experience and savor the fruits of this labor.

SELENITE

Purify yourself and connect to the higher energies always available to you.

DEAR SOUL, I INTRODUCE MYSELF, I AM THE SPIRIT OF selenite — ethereal white, gentle as a cuddle, yet at the same time strong and quick. I am connected to the special forces that, when required, come from Heaven, such as beings of light, angels, and ascended masters.

One of my qualities is to clean your aura — your electromagnetic field. Your aura presents in iridescent colors and can get dirty like clothes you never wash. As this happens over time, you can generate and manifest physical discomfort, even to the point of fatigue. We are here to intervene at various energetic levels of your body to restore your mental clarity and physical strength. Now, the need is to cleanse and strengthen your overall body system. Ask for Heaven's intervention and support to reconnect you with your inner light. I am your staunchest ally, along with the spirits of light who help anyone seeking to nurture their energetic wellbeing. I can support practitioners or therapists from any field, and be a tool for clients before therapy, empathizing with them and facilitating.

You can use me as a magic wand to cleanse and strengthen a person's aura. The intention is to remove the polluted veil that blocks the vision of truth. Before you drift into slumber, request permission to rest on a selenite cradle, granting me and the benevolent spirits of light the opportunity to purify and link you to the dream realm, our abode, where we can convey messages to your soul. Remember that I, by my constitution, do not like water so much. You can regenerate me by exposing me to the light of the new, crescent, and full moon.

May this gentle shower of light cleanse away all the burdens that obscure your innate radiance. We hold affection for you, stand by your side, and aspire for your aura to grow vast and resilient, enabling you to shine without constraint.

SMOKY QUARTZ

New cycles of life await you,
follow the path that shows you the light.

DEAR SOUL, IT IS THE LIGHT BEING OF SMOKY QUARTZ that speaks with you. I bring with me royalty, grandeur, and strength. I come to you now to tell you this — remember your strength, do not be afraid. I know you are tired; the road has been long. You've faced many challenges, but now I'm here to lend you support, along with my wise friend, the eagle owl. Their eyes shine like lighthouses, providing wisdom and light in the darkest of times. Even in the depths of night, remember to kindle a light to dispel the fear of darkness.

We are here at this time to help you reflect and become aware of yourself. It is true, you have suffered at times—even physically—but you have gone beyond that. What warrior does not suffer in his training? Life can be like a tunnel, especially during moments when we feel more fragile. It can feel like we're trapped in a spiral that never seems to end, where everything keeps repeating itself. Here, you are approaching the exit, but your strength is needed. Facing what you're going through is something you can't afford not to do. Only within your experience can you regain awareness, bringing light to all your resistances so that you can dissolve them and become stronger. This is where to go from here.

I invite you to take a moment of reflection. Take hold of this card and let yourself be transported into it, almost hypnotically. Breathe slowly and deeply, at least three or four times. Let go of your resistance and listen to how you are inside. We are here with you. We can be supportive. Remember to regain your strength, nourish yourself with joy, and dance inside that tunnel because soon another cycle of life will begin.

Carry me as jewelry or as a meditation partner. My work is not immediate, I need time. When we have finished our passage together, you will let me go. I ask you to wash and bless me by leaving me exposed to the sunlight to recharge.

Our friend owl and I bid you farewell, sending you light and wishing that your journey will make you stronger and more self-aware.

SNOWFLAKE OBSIDIAN

Change and transformation must be
sustained with strength.

WELCOME, DEAR SOUL, I AM THE SPIRIT OF SNOWFLAKE obsidian. The fire of the earth resides within me, and strength and transformation are my watchwords. I arrive after an explosion in which inevitable change becomes beauty. Accompanying me is none other than the sacred phoenix. Her story is legendary, as she is reborn from her own ashes, stronger than before.

We understand that you're emerging from a challenging—at times burdensome—phase, and you desire a complete transformation of your life. A restlessness shakes you inside, and you find yourself continually assessing what's right or wrong. If you want real, generative change, you have to let go — in the true sense of the word. Let go of all the memories of past hurts that have conditioned your present self. Take back your life with a new awareness. You have learned a lot from what was and become strong. Let go, let go ...

Dear warrior soul, letting go does not mean erasing or forgetting, but becoming aware of your strength and changing accordingly, putting it into action in your daily life. I know we are asking a lot of you, but you are ready. You must know that this is the right time for you to regain your strength of soul. It already resides within you. I know change is always scary, but you can allow yourself to go beyond that and live a full, rewarding, and challenging life.

I am black and white in color, reminding you that both darkness and light are part of you. It is important that you are aware of both so you know your personal characteristics. Don't keep judging yourself, you will only waste energy and produce fear. We are here to protect and support you through your metamorphosis. Don't make any hasty decisions until you understand the work you need to do on yourself. Focus on your regenerative strength. When you regain clarity, then you can move.

Carry me with you throughout the day. Meditating with me will let you touch your dark sides and help you sustain them. When I need a recharge, wash me under water and expose me to sunlight.

We hope that you express your strength in tangible ways and that your evolution unfolds like wonderful fireworks, allowing you to be proud of yourself.

SODALITE

Be free to express who you really are
by following your truth.

SOUNDS OF DRUMS ... VOICES SINGING ... DANCERS manifesting around the fire ... the howling of wolves echoing the ceremonial hymn of releasing true essence under the starlit sky ... the freedom to be oneself regardless of the judgment of others. I am the spirit of sodalite. Come to me; liberate and transform your ego into a communication that is constructive, authentic, and serene, first and foremost to you.

The time has come for each spirit to express their unique mode of communication, even in silence, radiating its inherent beauty. It's not about domination, manipulation, or persuasion, but about conveying words of light. Cleanse and celebrate the knots in your throat, your fears, and the sense of inadequacy — all of this is created by you, and it is your responsibility to take care of it. The situations you have experienced in the past have conditioned you, which is why it is essential to cleanse and rediscover who you really are. Release the tension on your shoulders, free your voice and find your song, rest in your silence and listen deep within — there you will find your truth.

The wolves, my friends, are present to convey that your fear of their strength may be unwarranted. Have you ever contemplated that they could, in fact, be your friends and allies? They might offer lessons in self-loyalty and the freedom to manifest. Celebrate your free spirit today, sing, and resonate like the sound of the drum within you. Together with us, decide to take responsibility for what you say and how you say it, because many situations and relationships in your life could change.

When you carry me, wear me close to your throat, sleep with me, or meditate with me, immersed inside my blue-and-white-striped color. I will lead you into the immensity of existence.
I, the spirit of sodalite, in the company of the wolves, wish for you to celebrate your true self, and may your journey be a liberating melody.

SUNSTONE

Rest and remember to regain the balance of your inner sun.

I AM THE SPIRIT OF THE SUNSTONE. MY COLORS REMIND you how much I can warm and recharge you in times of need. Masculine energy resides in me, and that is why I create movement. The ancient world believed that I came from the stars after a lunar eclipse.

I am in the company of my sacred tiger friend — proud, strong, and imposing. With great beauty, her stride is slow and elegant. When she hunts, she is fast and unerring. But even a splendid tiger, brimming with its primal strength, cannot risk hunting without sufficient nourishment and rest, as it may fall prey to a stronger predator. With that, I remind you that the sun god sustains you by giving you abundance and prosperity.

Dear soul, residing in human form as you are, you should know that there is a sun within you constantly nourishing and harmonizing with your physiology. It is an important flame that must be kept in balance. Like the sun, you need to follow a natural cycle of day and night, activity and rest. Recently, you have been neglecting this cycle. Your whole body needs to rest. We bring you a warning — you cannot afford to act or make decisions in your daily life if you are tired or drawing on your vital energy reserves. This makes you lose the lucidity of knowing where to go and what to do.

Everything seems to escape you, but it does not — it's only your physical state that is making you believe this. Now, it is essential that you rest. The night will regenerate what you need to do in the day. We advise you to help your physiology by cleansing with herbal teas, decoctions, or energized water. You can also stay in the sun or walk gently in nature. Give yourself time, refocus this force residing in you, and imagine for a moment what would happen if the sun did not exist. Everything around you would be dead and devoid of color.

Carry me with you during the day and place me in the center of your body — I will help you. I love to be washed and charged in the sun, when you feel I need it.

We wish for the sun to be a constant source of sustenance and guidance in your life, illuminating your path.

TIGER'S EYE

Stand up for and pursue your choices
with confidence and character.

I AM THE SPIRIT OF TIGER'S EYE AND I WELCOME YOU, dear soul. My strength lies in presence, awareness, intelligence, independence, and practicality in dealing with life's situations. Here with me are my sacred cat friends, and we wish to tell you something important.

You're influenced by others' opinions due to a lack of self-confidence and a loss of clarity about your own desires. External judgments or doubts about your life can reduce your energy, leading to mood swings and racing thoughts. We invite you to stop. You need to rebalance your energy and clarify your thoughts. It may be helpful to isolate yourself for a while and reflect.

We don't care if you choose what's 'right' or 'wrong', as long as you choose for yourself. Your decisions about who you are and what will happen will only lead to growth. Your path is unique to you. Whatever potholes or hiccups you may find will be exactly what you need to evolve. No one can decide for you. If you decide to stay where you are, it is your choice. But you will always be at the mercy of others' whims.

Our cat friends bring their attitude as a gift to you. They are their own masters. They decide who to be with and come and go when they want. They convey the energy of the places where they live and are natural cleaners. They will teach you the art of the equilibrist who knows how to stand between two forces. Regain your independence and self-confidence to feel better.

As a stone, I am quite solitary, and due to my innate need for independence, I prefer to be carried alone, just like cats who are irreverent and free. Keep me with you during the day and I will help balance your energy. Let me be with you in your workspace and I will support you to be independent. Put me back at night, as I like the solace of the dark. Wash me with water and rest me in the sun a whole day so that I can recharge myself.

We wish for you to regain your energy, so you can walk proudly and confidently, independent and self-assured.

TOURMALINATED QUARTZ

Align your destiny with the guidance of neutrality.

WELCOME, DEAR SOUL, WE ARE THE SPIRITS OF tourmalinated quartz. We are twins born without sex for a specific reason. Father Sky has designed us this way, intending for us to bring a realignment that can aid those who seek to harmonize their masculine and feminine aspects. Our purpose is to remind you to step out of the world of polarity, and to feel neutral, balanced, and aware that you are a precious star in the universe. A great principle we are bringing to you today, but I hope it all resonates loud and clear within you.

Many situations recently have led you astray, and now the need is precisely to put you back on the line of your destiny. To do this, it is important that you stop and reflect and evaluate what you are experiencing by adopting a different outlook. Dear soul, ask yourself now, "Why have I been shaken so much by the situations I am experiencing? Why am I allowing this? What part of me is involved?" These are the questions you need to ask yourself honestly and lucidly in an emergency.

Light and dark — one cannot exist without the other. From what we take for granted, important reflections can sometimes arise. For example, to see the brightest stars, even the most distant ones, there has to be darkness. To recognize the things you need to value most, you need to be in situations where those things don't exist. Instead of running away, make friends with your darkness. Oh yes, we are here to remind you of this; what we call 'destiny' does not have a 'right' or 'wrong' side, but it contains the meaning of path and choice. Therefore, get to work on your uncomfortable edges and embrace them for what they are with acceptance. It is not an easy task — we are the clear quartz and the black tourmaline born together. This should give you an idea of how important it is that you take charge of your destiny, because only then will you feel the strength that can arise when our two parts walk together.

Imagine that you are like a tightrope walker, walking between two forces, but being dominated by neither. You are not in judgment or in conflict, but you offer them a glimpse by giving them a smile. If you can put this into action, you will gain the frequency of a star. Now, allow yourself to become great and find within yourself that neutrality. It will take time for this to settle in and work with all facets of your star-like being. It will be a lifelong journey, but one that can bring great satisfaction. If you wish, bring us along and we will help you feel you are in the right place at the right time. If you meditate with us, you will have a chance to meet us. If you wish to keep us in your home or workplace, we will ensure that these environments remain neutral. We will be at your service as often as you need us.

We hope that your journey, dear soul, is adorned with stars, allowing you to experience the beauty of a starry night within yourself.

TURQUOISE

The presence and wisdom of the heart
are one with the shamanic spirit.

DEAR SOUL, I AM THE SPIRIT OF THE TURQUOISE, AND with me is a family of beautiful dolphins. We are here to honor your unique and special frequency. You should know that many ancient texts speak of me. Stories are told of shamans, healers, witches, sorcerers, and great kings who wielded my stones. My colors are of the sea and sky, I am very ancient and deep, and I connect sounds and vibrations as a healing tool. I bring the courage and energy of a fearless soul into your heart. I will whisper the stories of women and men who were able to use this energy for the greater good, reminding you that you were one of them.

The leaps and songs of dolphins are meant to pay homage to the joy in seeing you today. They are here to give you their intelligence, tenderness, and family union so that your heart may awaken fearless and full of the knowledge that you belong to our family from the stars. Through song and dance, the earth celebrates, reverberating in the depths of the cosmic waters.

Dear soul, you are precious to us, and the world needs your presence. The awakening of your ancient memories as a healer connected to Mother Earth gives you the physical and spiritual strength you seek. Your soul is ancient, carrying a wealth of experiences and talents within. Whatever your art, express it in your daily life. I sense that you acknowledge your uniqueness in the way you perceive and envision life. It's crucial to realize that you shouldn't suppress this distinctiveness. Your soul was born free, and the more you stifle it, the more complexities will arise in your life.

Today we want to give you one more splendid gift, which comes from your loving and supportive ancestors — a precious cloak. Imagine wearing it whenever you want to connect with us. It will protect you and give you the ability to talk to us and receive our advice. You can also utilize it to simply tap into that heart energy that makes you feel at home. Remember that a true healer is one who is healed and is in service, connecting with Heaven and Earth. Now it's your turn to continue your healing journey.

Surround yourself with like-minded people, kind of like a soul family, because unity is strength, and you need that. Be strong when you have to make choices for yourself. Remember to listen to yourself, but at the same time open up fearlessly, confident that you can do it.

I will be happy to support you when I am on your person. When you wish to recharge me, you should know that I am sensitive to sunlight, so wash me and expose me outdoors, but in the shade.

We wish for you to experience life in a way that allows you to freely manifest who you are: a soul healed from personal wounds, ready to offer its presence and whatever else you choose to become.

WATERMELON TOURMALINE

Honor your empathy and let love
flow without attachment.

DEAR SPECIAL SOUL, WELCOME! I AM THE SPIRIT OF watermelon tourmaline and various layers and shades of color live within me. I provide protection, support, and deep listening. I know that love made of empathy and truth called 'friendship' is a truly precious treasure.

Today, dear soul, I come to caress your heart and point out how many different aspects of love there are. Sincere and selfless love comes from the ability to release ourselves from all forms of possession, attachments, and jealousy toward someone else. Understand that to do this, your inner, mental, and emotional layers must be detached. Whenever you are afraid of losing someone—whether it is a love affair, a friend, or a relationship with a family member—you hide behind your need to be loved. It is as if you are metaphorically slapping yourself in the face. Instead, I am here to caress you, and whisper to you to overcome the fears of abandonment and to understand that they don't really exist. Deep love is without possession. If you keep this in mind, you will no longer feel abandoned or betrayed.

You must know that at a higher level, love is eternal. In earthly life, made up of a thousand situations and multiple choices, paths may part but that is certainly not why you stop loving. If you can approach and reach this higher level of love, you will make yourself and those around you free. At the same time, you will be inhabited by immense love.

With me are three sacred hares, reminding you of lightheartedness, play, and observation. They know when to get away from dangerous situations, which may present to you as emotional addictions. They roam freely, then return independently and unrestrained. Together, we aim to shield and bolster you with a genuine embrace, bestowing upon you a profound sensation of surrender, free from any mental preconceptions regarding its significance or expected reciprocity.

Free yourself from the idea of love itself and how you were taught it. I know you might be thinking about loneliness right now, and that your mind struggles to grasp certain concepts, but don't get lost there — that's just your fears and neediness talking. You are a good friend, and your empathy allows you to speak the truth with love. Remain non-attached to this beauty and use it. Vibrate, dear soul, like a heart free from conditioning.

I can stay with you as long as you wish and help sustain your layers and savor them. You can wash me with water and expose me to sunlight or moonlight, depending on what you feel in your heart.

We sincerely desire that your life is abundant in this liberated and wholesome love, transforming it into something divine.

WHITE LABRADORITE

Allow yourself to manifest your magic.

DEAR SOUL, WELCOME. AN ANCIENT MAGIC RESIDES IN me. I am the spirit of white labradorite, and I can be extremely charming and sweet. My white-witch personality allows me to remove the veils of illusions that you often create for yourself in daily life. My color is white with rainbow highlights. I can work with you and on you on various layers because I cover a wide energy spectrum. The energy knows exactly where it needs to go, regardless of what we do.

I come to you together with the majestic white deer, an animal that evokes fairy tales and stories of yesteryear, representing purity, strength, and wisdom. If you should encounter them in one of your visions, bow down before them because they carry great teachings. The white candle is pure magic, rich in memories.

We are here to tell you that you need magic in your life. Your potential allows for it, but you are lost in the meanderings of your personality. Your vision is limited, your eyes fixated solely on the reality of only what you can touch. But there is much more to this world.

Why is it beneficial to discard the illusions and self-created stories? Deceivers are ever-present, and while you're navigating life without full engagement, you become more susceptible to manipulation. This is not your potential. I realize that it is easier to conform to everyone else's thinking, but please understand how much of a waste this behavior is for the good of humanity.

In my world, beauty is authentic, simple, and in balance. In your world, on the other hand, beauty is constrained by canon and rules constructed only to manipulate. This is where you must not fail, because you do not need to dissipate your beauty.

With us you can find an ancient connection that helps bring back a deep sense of gratitude and trust in something greater. Your experiences will be elevated to a higher level. Immerse yourself in the beauty and poetry of this card. Listen on a deeper level, and you will discover how sensuality and feminine energy will strengthen your sensibilities. I may not be immediately understandable because I work through the reflections of a multifaceted image, breaking through everything you see. One thing is clear, however — I cannot make you see things differently unless you are the first to wish it. That is the choice you will have to make.

We can work with you by day and by night, where we will take you into the dream world to find advice and memories as you slumber. My great connection to the moon allows me to act as a vehicle of your transformation for you, empowering you to connect and communicate with the spirits of nature and the unseen world. You can do this through whichever technique or practice resonates most — meditation, shamanic journeying, theta healing, visualization, etc.

Wash me with a little water and then expose me to the light of the full or crescent moon when you wish. Look at the mirror of your life and see how many reflections you have in front of you. Remove one layer at a time, what is superfluous will rise to the surface from time to time.

We hope that the magic returns and allows the white witch or sorcerer within you to emerge.

THE DIRECTIONS CARD MESSAGES

EASTERN DIRECTION

New adventures await you.

A NEW SUN AND A NEW DAWN ARISE FOR YOU TODAY, dear soul. I am the force that drives renewal. I open the door to new things, and I create enthusiasm to pursue your dreams. You are ready for my energy: the direction of east.

Do not be afraid. I am here to give you an injection of confidence. Open your eyes wide and full of wonder. Along with me comes a beautiful stork and the crystals of aventurine, aquamarine, and fluorite. They come to remind you of the beauty in observing a new birth and the adrenaline rush of feeling alive. Their message is the possibility of creating who you are in constant renewal.

If you feel it, perform a ritual to help train yourself to express your heart's desires. Wait until the waxing crescent moon and write a clear and precise wish on a sheet of paper. This can be something you want to renew about yourself, a project you would like to see come to fruition, or anything else. Remember to say thank you and sign the paper. Find a shelf that faces east and will not be disturbed, because your wish will have to remain exposed until the full moon. Place one or all three of these crystals with a pink candle on top of the paper. It can remain lit during this time (always within safe limits, of course). You may also choose to enrich this space with flowers or herbs — I will be very happy, because I like these very much.

Face eastward and read your wish aloud each night. Light the candle, feeling a great sense of confidence arise in you that something new approaches. This process should be inaugurated on the first day of the waxing crescent moon and repeated every day until the full moon — only then can you burn your paper because your wish will have arrived loud and clear to the Creator Universe.

We hope each new day amazes you as you renew yourself with the rising dawn.

NORTHERN DIRECTION

Stop and listen to your inner voice.

WELCOME, DEAR SOUL, TO THE DIRECTION OF NORTH. Turn your gaze northward. Currently, the energy flowing through your life can assist you in detaching from situations, experiences, or rigid thoughts that lack vision.

I am a strong energy — full of wisdom and listening, cooling the most restless spirits. A beautiful white bear is here, along with the energy of hyaline quartz, selenite, and apophyllite. They serve as a reminder of the importance of retreating into deep listening, practicing silence and meditation at this time. It is necessary to have the strength and wisdom of the bear

— they know how to retreat when they must. Heaven and its messengers want to support you. You are a precious soul to us all. Do not be afraid of loneliness because, in reality, you are never alone.

I want to leave you today with a precious ritual you can practice over a whole lunar cycle. Wait for the waning moon — we need this energy to help you let go. Take any of these three crystals, a white candle, and this card. Place everything somewhere they will not be disturbed, facing north. On a blank piece of paper, write a request for help to let something go. Say thank you and sign your wish, a gesture of the responsibility you will take for working together with us. Every night until the moon has completely set, light the candle (if possible, make sure it stays lit all night, making it safe), observe this card and read your intention, feeling it flow through you. As time passes, you should feel an increased sense of lightness as you let go of any kind of expectation, as you trust the energies of the universe will support you. As we learn to accept, we learn to flow in harmony with higher frequencies which will lead us to be more attuned to our higher self. The more we practice being in this state of allowance, the more we will notice things beginning to fall into place effortlessly.

We hope that life reminds you of the importance of nurturing and honoring your soul.

SOUTHERN DIRECTION

Have the courage to manifest your sunshine.

I AM THE SPIRIT OF THE SOUTHERN DIRECTION. STRONG and impetuous, the fire of manifestation resides within me. I do not know the word 'surrender' because I represent constant resilience. I manifest through the energy of creativity, building steadily every day. I give energy and strength to face what life presents with open arms.

Here with me today are the strength and wonder of bees, skilled in building something perfect and nourishing — pure, poured gold. Their lesson concerns the patience and perseverance needed to build something important. Citrine quartz, sunstone and tiger's eye protect you and inspire you to go beyond your limits and shine like a true sun.

All these forces live within you — you simply need the courage to manifest them. With the energy of the new moon, I invite you to perform a ritual that will give you the boost you need. Find a southward-facing surface on which you can place the tools you need. Take an orange candle, an amount of honey and olive oil each in a small glass or jar.

Write down a clear intention of what you would like to manifest, sign it, and say thank you as an act of awareness. After that, take ten minutes to read your intention, breathing slowly from your abdomen. Turn your hands toward the two vessels containing the oil and honey and visualize a beautiful golden light charging these beautiful gifts of Mother Nature with energy. You will be able to take advantage of their charged goodness by consuming them in the following days. Take deep breaths feeling a sense of immense gratitude in your heart for this wonderful gift.

We hope you become a radiant sun, where your determination and enthusiasm become valuable assets in your life.

WESTERN DIRECTION

Embrace the unknown and abandon resistance.

I LIVE IN THE SETTING SUN, PAINTING THE SKY with colors that make your eyes shine. Alongside, I carry transformation and release in the embrace of the unknown. I can give you a point of deep observation, and—like a blank sheet of paper—readiness for anything.

I am the direction of west, and I realize I create a certain awe given my strength. The approaching darkness has always sparked stories and fears among humans, simply because they cannot explain what they feel.

Dear soul, knowing what tomorrow holds is a mere illusion of the controlling mind. Allow every cell within you to vibrate with the knowledge that anything can happen. And you will be able to cope with anything serenely, thanks to your strength. Focus on the beautiful things that can surprise you. The snowflake obsidian, rhodonite, and moonstone crystals are here to help you through this beautiful transformation. The strong dragon, proud and imposing, reminds you how ancient your soul is. A special flame burns within you — work on it so that you can manifest it.

This ritual honors the powerful force residing within you. With the energy of a full moon night, find a westward-facing shelf and place a purple candle. Take this card and place it next to the candle, along with a glass jug filled with water. Around this, place the three crystals related to this card. Finally, take a piece of paper and write on it what you wish to transform or manifest about yourself. Sign it off with gratitude, because you are making a commitment. When you feel ready, light the candle and reread what you wrote, invoking the west and feeling the dragon blood flowing within you. The following day, burn your note and drink the water, which will be charged with the energy of this ritual and the full moon. Then let everything go to what will be.

We hope you harness your transformative power at the right moments, relishing your motivation to approach each day with fresh intent.

WHITE FEATHER

All doors are open before you.

WELCOME DEAR SOUL. IF YOU COME TO ME TODAY IT IS because you have a thousand possibilities before you. I represent the spirit of they who are able to fly. I let myself go with extreme softness, letting the wind rock me. I do not judge what happens to me but act accordingly. Universal forces guide me.

If you come across me near a tree, by the roadside, or anywhere your path leads you, take me as a sign of something hidden from your eyes, yet deeply present, embracing your heart.

Your motto for today is:

You can — but only if you want to!

You are not alone, you have support, but you just have to decide what you want most. You need to seek motivation and clarity. Your paper is blank, an empty canvas just waiting for you.

Have faith in your destiny, no matter how heavy it is. What matters is how you decide to deal with it. The soul does not know what human emotions are. It has the need to evolve from its memories to return to the origin. Have faith in it.

I hope a gentle feather will grace your face during an unexpected moment, opening doors to countless possibilities ahead.

ABOUT THE AUTHOR

BARBARA MARCHI is a lifelong crystal enthusiast who's had a deep connection with these radiant gems since her earliest days. Back in 2001, she realized her dream by opening the enchanting KIRA store in Verona. It's become a haven where Barbara shares her two-decades-strong expertise in the world of crystal healing, making their powerful messages accessible to all.

Barbara's journey led her to explore shamanism and immerse herself in the transformative practice of Polarity Therapy. Now, she uses this wealth of knowledge to offer individual and group sessions, guiding people toward expanded awareness and profound transformation.

Not only is Barbara a crystal connoisseur, she's also a collaborator. She's worked alongside biologist-musician Emiliano Toso and filmmaker Thomas Torelli, expanding her horizons and bringing her unique insights to a broader audience.

Join her on a journey of self-discovery and healing through the world of crystals and energy at **kiraoggettidalmondo.com** or on Instagram **@negozio_kira** or **barbara_esperienze_dicristallo**.

ABOUT THE ARTIST

Step into the world of **CRISTINA FONTANA**, a lifelong lover of art, illustration, and the mystique of the invisible. With a master's degree in hand, she initially delved into the world of the theater in Vicenza, Italy, focusing on the captivating realm of entertainment communication.

Cristina's journey took an intriguing turn as she ventured into the study of shamanism. This marked the beginning of her continuous exploration into holistic disciplines, as she sought new avenues for personal growth and awareness. Today, she's chosen to reignite her true passion—art—blending it seamlessly with the wisdom she's gathered along the way.

A fateful encounter with Barbara several years back sparked the flame of collaboration. The result? The remarkable *Shamanic Crystals Oracle* project, born from their shared vision of providing individuals with a powerful tool for inner growth.

Join Cristina on her social media as she weaves her artistic talents into a tapestry of spiritual insight and holistic wellbeing:

Instagram: **cristinaliliafontana**
Facebook: **Cristina Lilia Fontana**

ALSO AVAILABLE FROM BLUE ANGEL PUBLISHING®

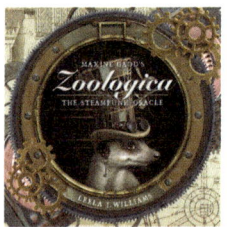

Maxine Gadd's Zoologica: The Steampunk Oracle

Leela J. Williams
Artwork by Maxine Gadd

In the imaginative realm of the Zoologica, peculiar tales, alchemical insights and unusual wisdoms merge into profound meaning, remarkable understanding and empowered transformations. Here, shifting gears and pivoting cogs become components of your chosen destiny.

Shuffle the cards to enter a liminal landscape where divinatory gadgets and looking-glass wonders reveal hidden realities and possibilities. See the past, present and future with clarity and discover tools for accepting, refining and reinventing their pathways.

Go deep into your questioning, illuminate shadows, shift the gears of probability and further your fantastic journey of self-engineered actualisation.

40 CIRCULAR CARDS AND 144-PAGE FULL-COLOUR GUIDEBOOK.
ISBN: 978-1-922573-97-1

ALSO AVAILABLE FROM BLUE ANGEL PUBLISHING®

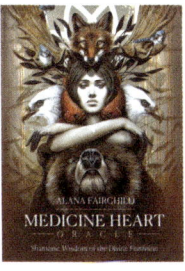

Medicine Heart Oracle
Shamanic Wisdom of the Divine Feminine

Alana Fairchild
Artwork by Sophie Wilkins

Connect with the eternal essence of Mother Earth to honour the natural wisdom and loving intelligence of your Medicine Heart. Within the soul-nurturing space of this sacred oracle, you will discover precious offerings nestled in seen and unseen dimensions. Breathe into your questioning and allow shamanic treasures from around the globe to reveal ancient pathways, creative visions and potent spirituality. You are ready to vitalise your transformational purpose, so move with the healing rhythms of Earth and Sky and enrich your life for the benefit of all.

Beloved human, may your Medicine Heart be infused with divine blessings and benefits, and your swift and complete fulfilment generate joy and unity for all beings.

44 CARDS + 368-PAGE FULL-COLOUR GUIDEBOOK.
ISBN: 978-1-922573-80-3

ALSO AVAILABLE FROM BLUE ANGEL PUBLISHING®

The Angel Magic Oracle
Empowering Guidance & Divine Love

Tess Whitehurst
Artwork by Jessica von Braun

Angel magic is accessible to all who seek it. In this ethereal oracle, you have a direct link to the boundless support, insight, and blessings of the celestial realms. Hold the deck to your heart to align yourself with the luminous presence of the angels. Welcome their energy as you shuffle and choose your cards. The big questions and the small ones are received by the angels with love, so you always receive wise, relevant, and practical responses in accord with your highest healing, purpose, and possibility.

Angels appear in ways that resonate with our souls and make our consciousness sing. When we are open to their tenderness, we can experience our divinity and know the truth of their guidance through our own awakening.

56 CARDS + 144-PAGE FULL-COLOUR GUIDEBOOK.
ISBN: 978-1-922573-93-3

ALSO AVAILABLE FROM BLUE ANGEL PUBLISHING®

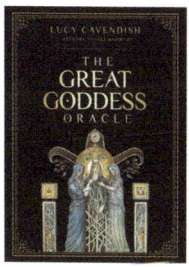

THE GREAT GODDESS ORACLE

LUCY CAVENDISH
ARTWORK BY JAKE BADDELEY

Profound and transformative, diverse and empowering, the many faces of the Great Goddess have nurtured and guided our souls across lifetimes. This inspiring new oracle from Lucy Cavendish and Jake Baddeley will draw the manifold Maiden, Mother, and Crone closer, rekindling the eternal light of the sacred feminine within you. With every card, you will receive loving guidance, enduring strength and timeless wisdom.

The Great Goddess is the eternal dance separating and harmonising the forces of chaos and order within the cosmos. Be moved by Her wonder, be guided by Her prophecy. Speak her invocations, receive her blessings, and walk the true path of your beautiful soul.

42 CARDS + 168-PAGE FULL-COLOUR GUIDEBOOK.
ISBN: 978-1-922573-99-5

NOTES

NOTES

NOTES

NOTES

For more information on this
or any Blue Angel Publishing release,
please visit our website at:

www.blueangelonline.com